I0478692

Investing For Beginners: The Ultimate Investing Guide for Newbies

How To Confidently Manage And Grow Your Money Successfully

By

Michele Gilbert

<u>Visit My Amazon Author Page</u>

Dedicated to those who choose to stretch beyond their own limits and to seek a more abundant and fulfilling life.

Your thoughts are creative.

Michele Gilbert

My Free Gift To You!

As a way of saying thank you for downloading my book, I am willing to give you access to a selected group of readers who (every week or so) receive inspiring, life-changing kindle books at deep discounts, and sometimes even absolutely free.

Wouldn't it be great to get amazing Kindle offers delivered directly to your inbox?

Wouldn't it be great to be the first to know when I'm releasing new fresh and above all sharply discounted content?

But why would I do something like this?

Why would I offer my books at such a low price and even give them away for free when they took me countless hours to produce?

Simple…. Because I Want To Spread The Word.!

For a few short days Amazon allows Kindle authors to promote their newly released books by offering them deeply discounted (up to 70% price discounts and even for free. This allows us to spread the word extremely quickly allowing users to download thousands and thousands of copies in a very short period of time.

Once the timeframe has passed, these books will revert back to their normal selling price. That's why you will benefit from being the first to know when they can be downloaded for free!

So are you ready to claim your weekly Kindle books?

You are just one click away! Follow the link below and sign up to start receiving awesome content

Thank you and Enjoy!

Table of contents

Introduction

I want to thank you and congratulate you for downloading the book, "

Investing For Beginners: The Ultimate Investing Guide For Newbies

This book contains proven steps and strategies on *How to Confidently Manage and Grow Your Money Successfully*

Are you fed up with the traditional 9 to 5 job? Do you want to earn more money fast? What is the best way to secure your financial independence? What is passive income? What is the secret behind successful investors? If you want to learn more about successful investment decisions than you should read this book.

Thanks again for downloading this book, I hope you enjoy it!

After studying the work of the world's biggest investors I have decided to summarize the most important investment decisions of these individuals. I have noticed that most of them have followed the same pattern and most of these successful individuals have the same mindset.

I knew about this type of mindset long before studying the works of these people and the mindset is what sets successful people apart from unsuccessful people. I am confident that when you will reach the end of this book your view on financial investment will be completely changed.

I wrote this book in order to teach the average American about the core principles of successful investment. After struggling with a traditional 9 to 5 job I have realized that the best way to secure my financial independence would be through saving money and making wise investment decisions.

This book was created for people who are looking to become successful investors and the main purpose of this book is to give you an insight in the most essential rules of successful investment. If you read this book you will be able to discover new opportunities of investment and you will master the art of generating passive income from your investment

Chapter 1

The Best Way to Save Money for Your Investment

The first thing that you need to understand is that saving money is a essential skill and it takes a lot of time to perfect. You can start by saving $50/month and then you can increase your sum to $100/month. It is extremely important to save money because every dollar that you save will bring you closer to your dream of financial independence.

We live in a world where there is a huge temptation to waste money. This is why the vast majority of people end up poor – they cannot save money. Every dollar that is not saved will eventually lead to just another missed opportunity and in order to become successful you will have to save money on a daily basis. Moreover you will also have to come up with a mindset that will help you to make more money but I will explain that later on in my book.

The best way to save money is by taking 20% of your income and saving it into an account which is destined for financial accumulation. If you are able to save just $50/month and if you invest that money in an average mutual fund you will be able to earn $50000 in just 10 years.

The most amazing fact about saving money is that even by saving a few dollars/day you can achieve financial independence. There are so many ways to make money these days and the sad reality is that in order to make money you need to spend some money.

I know that a lot of people do not like this idea but this is the most important fact. If you are not able to save a few dollars you will never have the money which you may need to test out new markets or new types of revenue generating possibilities. Even if you earn the minimum wage you can become rich if you are willing to save money for a prolonged period of time.

It is not easy to develop this lifelong habit of saving and investing money yet the rewards are well worth it if you are willing to put in the effort. This sort of effort requires tremendous determination and willpower because you need to make a goal out of your decision and you need to stick to that goal every day but if you get used to this practice your financial success will be guaranteed.

The key is to practice frugality on a daily basis. You will need to question every expenditure and you should delay any sort of buying decision. Most people stay poor because they have this impulsive desire to spend money and burn it all down but this is exactly the opposite of what you need to do in order to raise the necessary capital funds for your investment.

Chapter 2

Financial Planning Tips & Tricks

If you want to become financially independent you need to follow a set of rules and you need to discipline yourself in order to respect your rules on a daily basis. The most important rule is to spend less than you earn. If you manage to do this you will be able to invest the rest of your money and you will start to earn more money. This is one of the oldest rules in the world and it has never failed.

The toughest part of saving money involves your personal status. You will have to make a lot of sacrifices in terms of lifestyle but these sacrifices may prepare you for a frugal life. You will have to stop buying new clothes or other things that will make you feel good temporarily but will eventually end up by ruining your savings budget.

One of the most important rules is to never touch the money. If you have placed the money away into a savings account you should never touch this money. A lot of people think that if they save money they can eventually spend that money. If you are tempted to spend money you should create a separate account for spending money on the things that you love.

You will also have to form this habit of saving money and you will need to save money from the beginning of your career until the end of your working life. If you are able to do this you will have multiple funds to invest throughout your lifetime. This rule is a bit tough because you will have to live with 90% of your salary but if you practice this rule you will have a lot to gain.

The vast majority of people love to burn their money away and if they have something left they just place it in the bank for a short amount of time. After that time is gone they will get the money from the bank and they will spend it as well. You will also have to make sure to practice this rule of saving money on a daily basis. For every dollar saved there is a potential of doubling it in a medium time frame.

All in all, in order to become a successful financial planner you need to start by setting out goals on a daily basis and you need to be extremely frugal on a daily basis. If you manage to do this on a daily basis you will always have some money that you may use for small or medium sized investments and this is in fact the most important thing that you need to do in order to become a successful investor.

Chapter 3

Understanding the Law of Attraction and Multiplication

There is nothing in the world that is more fascinating than the law of attraction. This is how the Universe works and this is how things work in almost any aspect of life. Many financial scholars have talked about this law and they explained that if you save some money you can exploit new opportunities on the horizon.

It is as if this law was set out to bless the people who always have money but even the poor people may be able to benefit from this law if they are able to save money. There were times in my life when I had a lot of money and there were times when I had no money at all and when I had a lot of money I would make foolish decisions.

The most fascinating thing was that new opportunities for multiplication seemed to pop up when I had no more money at hand and this is why it is important for you to save because you can multiply that money in many ways. It is also important to understand that you need to have a mindset in order to exploit this law but even this is relatively easy to understand and I will explain this later on in my book.

The law of attraction is quite simple and it is based on real facts. Opportunities present themselves to people who are ready to take advantage of them and you cannot take advantage of any opportunity if you do not have the necessary financial resources or skills. These skills may revolve around the successful implementation of time management, financial planning and creativity.

You will need to be creative in order to expose the core of any business and you will have to realize that if you want to multiply your money you will have to work smarter, not harder. This is the most amazing thing in any business as there is always a way to work smarter and earns more. This is why the wealthiest people in the world work for a few hours a day because they know how to use time management creatively.

You will have to be creative in the multiplication process of your business and with the tools that you have available in this day and age it is easy to do that. There is this old saying that the money is in the list so create a list of customers or simply start by asking yourself every day about the things that you can do in order to multiply your earnings in an exponential manner. If you do this every day you will be amazed by the amount of money that you can eventually earn.

Chapter 4

Tips for Improving your Personality and Mindset

I have seen so many successful people and they all shared one thing in common – they had a fantastic mindset. They always saw an opportunity to generate income and invest that income and this is one of the most amazing things that I have witnessed. These people shared a positive personality and the word 'no' was not in their vocabulary.

A positive personality will have more influence on the results of your work and it will probably outweigh any other factor. To begin with it is important to understand that your physical diet has a huge impact on your health and personality. If you eat fresh food you will feel healthier and happier and this will help you in many ways.

In a somewhat similar fashion your mental diet defines your character and personality. When you feed your mind with positive ideas, information and positive thoughts you will be able to develop a more positive and constructive personality. You will become more influential and persuasive and you will enjoy your self confidence and self esteem.

Mental fitness is like physical fitness. You will start to develop high levels of self esteem and a positive mental attitude with training and practice. You will need to train your mind every day in order to become a completely positive person. If you manage to stay positive every day you will attract positive people around you and they will find pleasure in doing business with you.

There are several tricks that you can do in order to be a positive person. You can try to use positive self talk. You need to speak to yourself positively and control your inner dialogue. You will have to use positive statements about yourself and you should keep in mind that this is how positive people think most of the time.

Your inner thoughts will have a big impact on your actions and only if you remember this simple fact you will be able to focus more on your business and you will be able to grow your business in an exponential way. If you think every day about new ways of growing your business or new ways of saving money you will eventually be successful.

In the end it is important to remember that if you do not think positive you will fall into a trap that will make you to feel sad and you will worry a lot every day. Your mind needs to be filled with positive thoughts in order to eliminate the negative thoughts. If you do not take care of the information that goes through your mind you will start to develop a negative mindset.

Chapter 5

Understanding the Core Principles of Successful Investment Decisions

In order to make a wise investment decision you need to look at lots of things. You need to understand the fundamentals such as growth prospects. You need to understand the evaluation since you do not want to pay too much or you do not want to overlook a good value. You will also need to figure out more about what the market will say about the investment.

Most of the investors that I have met agree that fundamentals, evaluation and technical factors form the basis of a sound investment decision process but how they combine is a matter of much debate. Anyhow if you learn more about the fundamental aspects of investments the chances of making a bad investment will diminish greatly.

Sometimes the best thing that you can do is to keep things simple. If you see a return for you dollar you may already know that you took a wise investment decision. You should also try to focus on the overall price of your investment instead of speculating. It is also important to believe in your vision and stop believing in what other people tell you because you may end up confused.

It is also wise to understand the fact that 80% of your activities account for 20% of your results and those 80% of your activities may take up to 90% of your time. The starting point is to ask what are your most successful products and services. You will also need to find out who are your most successful customers and clients.

If you manage to find out what are the things that will give you the highest return on the amount of time and money that you invest you will eventually boost your income in an exponential manner. You will need to focus on the 20% and discontinue the activities that make up to 80% of your time.

You will also have to make a list of everything that you do in a week or a month. If you get that list and extract four things you will be quite surprised to see that those four things will amount to 90% of your total income. If you select one of those things you will eventually see that you have the answer to your biggest problem.

A successful investment also requires preparation. You need to learn how to use your pessimism in a positive way so start by thinking every day about the things that can go wrong in your business. If you develop this habit you will manage to avoid unexpected incidents that may completely destroy your investment.

Chapter 6

Generating Passive Income from Your Investment

When it comes to making money, passive income is definitely the way to go. There are many ways to make money but the fundamental purpose of any investment should be to generate passive income or in other words – make money even when you sleep.

In many businesses you will see that the top earners or the people, who earn the most money, are literally obsessed with passive income. They think day and night about new ways and methods that they can use in order to generate more and more passive income.

Let's say that you start a business by making T-shirts, you will eventually be successful because you will build a brand and you will manage to stand out with your brand. You can then delegate responsibility to another person and he will take over your business.

The key to generating passive income lies in the successful delegation of responsibility. This is not an easy thing to do because sometimes it may take years for you to learn the tips and tricks that may guarantee success in your business. If you learn how to delegate responsibility you can use the rest of your time to create a new business and generate a new stream of passive income.

Furthermore, if you manage to build a successful business model you will eventually manage to live your ideal life because this is the core principle of generating passive income anyway – who doesn't want to earn money while they are on vacation?

If you will strive to improve your business every single day you will manage to perfect your business model and you will have a successful business in a record time. This is what successful people do – they start up multiple businesses because they know the key principles for success in any business and they basically use the same principles over and over again.

In any business there is the core principle of momentum so if you start a business and if you persevere every day, you will keep on going faster and faster and your revenues will grow exponentially. At one point in time you will be motivated to start work earlier and to work harder, you will learn to prioritize and so on.

All in all, in order to generate passive income you must work hard and start by generating active income. You must then invest your active income in a business that allows you to grow your passive income potential in an unlimited manner. All in all, passive income is the best way to achieve financial freedom.

Chapter 7

Essential Tips for Long Term Investments

In order to benefit from long term investments you need to follow some basic rules. These rules were used by the most successful investors in the world and if you try to stick with these rules every day you will become a successful investor.

Monitoring your investment: This is one of the most important steps that you need to take in order to enjoy the benefits of a long term investment. You should never hurry and take the profit from an investment. You should also try to stop investing in things that do not bring immediate profit. In the world of investments you should never mix your emotions with certain stocks.

Start with a long term vision: It is always important to have a long term vision on things. If you start with a long term vision you will increase your chances for success. You need to stay strong and you must not panic when the market may crash. You should also try to sell your stocks if you are in desperate need of money, after all – you have started to invest in order to live an ideal life.

Diversification is the key for success: This is in fact one of the fundamental rules for safe investments. If you are able to diversify your investment portfolio you may achieve great success in your quest for financial independence.

Read: You will have to read as much as you can about new companies that may offer new investment opportunities. You will have to find a niche or an area where you have sufficient knowledge in order to exploit the actions of certain companies.

Risk: You need to think really well about the kind of risk that you are willing to take. Some people are capable of achieving great financial success because they know how to master the risks which are usually associated with a long term investment.

Time: Think about the amount of time that you may need to save the money for an investment. You should also think about the amount of time that you may need to recover the money from an investment. Some investments may help you to beat inflation while others will not even beat inflation and will turn out to be a disaster.

Work hard: You need to be willing to work hard in order to bring effective results to the table. You will have to decide about the amount of time that you may want to allocate to an investment and you must decide if you want to turn this into full time job or only a part-time activity.

Chapter 8

Tips & Tricks for Low Risk Investments

In order to find low risk investments you should be prepared to choose between owning money or lending money. Let's say that you have $1000 you may ask yourself: What can I do with this money? The answer is simple – you can either invest it or expect some return or you can have your own assets.

Besides the financial markets you should understand that there are multiple ways for investing your money. You can choose to invest in real estate or you might even try to invest in newly founded companies. You can buy stocks for companies that may bring in a fresh perspective on certain markets.

Either way, your biggest enemy is inflation and you should be prepared to fight inflation every day. You may also have long term investment plans and you may choose to invest in your retirement fund or in the education of your children. The bad news is that inflation can seriously affect these kinds of investments.

You should always try to exploit the time that you have at hand and you need to learn how to use your time in a wise manner. If you are young than you have a greater chance for success. Young people have enough time at hand in order to make wise investment decisions.

Another thing that you should consider is risk. You must understand that new opportunities may pop up on the horizon and you must be ready to take the risk and invest your money wisely. Moreover, if you diversify your investment portfolio you will have a greater chance of success. You must definitely try to invest in small amounts in order to boost your self-esteem.

It is always wise to choose safe investment opportunities even if they may not present so many benefits at first. They will at least offer you a safety net. You must also monitor your investments in a passive manner as if you monitor them too closely you may worry too much about your investment decisions. In order to make wise investment decisions you will need to learn how to delay gratification.

Furthermore, if you manage to delay gratification you will be able to enjoy the benefits from making long term investments and you will earn a sense of personal achievement that will encourage you to take on ever more challenging investment opportunities. All in all, if you are determined to make safe investments you should definitely take advantage of time, study the markets and prepare for a more frugal life.

Chapter 9
I hope this book was able to help you.

Your quest for achieving financial freedom through wise investment decisions is not an easy one to make. In the end, it is important to understand that the power of making wise investment decisions is in your hands and you are responsible for taking control of your life.

The most important fact is that you have been put in this world in order to do something wonderful with your life. You have a unique purpose in life but you need to self-manage that purpose and I truly believe that this book will help you to self-manage the most important purpose in your life.

Your role is to get on the road of becoming everything that you are capable of becoming. By taking charge of yourself you will begin to understand the fact that you are self-employed. You will understand that you will only work for yourself even if someone else signs your paycheck.

You must understand that you are the president of your own personal corporation and your duty is to go out into the marketplace and sell your products. The strongest people in the world are in complete charge of their destinies and they always operate their own corporation with the highest efficiency. If you will master the art of self-management you will be able to achieve everything that you have always wanted.

The next step is to understand the fact that you are your own boss even if you work for someone else. If you will follow the advice that I have presented in this book and if you apply it every day you will learn to manage and grow you're earning potential in an exponential fashion.

Conclusion

Thank you again for downloading this book!

I hope this book was able to help you learn the process for overcoming the fear of investing and help you to embark on a new financially free life.

The next step is to put these strategies into practice.

Before you go, I'd like to say thank you for purchasing my book.

I know you could have picked so many other books to read on the importance of overcoming insecurity and jealousy issues in your relationships. But you took a chance on me.

So A Big thanks for downloading this book and reading it all the way to completion.

Now I would like to ask a _small_ favor.

Could you please take a minute or two to leave a review for this book on Amazon?

Click here

The feedback will help me continue to publish more kindle books that will help people to get better results in their lives.

And if you found it helpful in anyway then please let me know :-)

Thank you and good luck!

Talk to the Hand

I don't know about you, but when I watch shows like *Lie to Me* or *Sherlock*, so often, I really, really wish that I could be that good. Heck, after I watched *The Mentalist* for the first time, I was studying everyone. I stared at footprints trying to see if I could tell whether the person walking was right handed or left handed. Not only is this super impractical for me as an actual skill, but it's super addicting. The thing is, it's all about studying people and watching them, but there's a science to it. I may not be out there catching criminals red handed for having a nervous tell, but it has helped me read situations and understand things that I previously missed.

So sure, you might not catch your arch-nemesis, but you might be able to understand things a little better with a little study of body language. And that's why I'm here. Body language is not just for detectives out there looking to catch murderers and thieves. Body language is the key to understanding the unspoken words that our body is communicating so heavily without our knowledge. Not only will this help you understand and relate to people better, but it'll make it so that you are aware of your own presence to others.

Nonverbal communication makes up the majority of our communication and most of us are clueless to the actual comprehension and understanding of it. That means that those who do not invest time in learning what to say in our nonverbal appearance are missing so much. But the truth is, we don't miss all of it. We have come to silently absorb and understand nonverbal communication, regardless of whether we know it or not. It's the art of learning to understand something we already know and to heighten our understanding and acceptance of what's being communicated to us. It's tricky, I know, but it's not impossible to understand.

What I'm going to tell you in this book is going to make sense to you and a lot of it is going to feel familiar, like you already knew that. Well, the reason for that is that you you've been picking up these silent transmissions for years, you just haven't acknowledged them or put a name to some of the habits you've already taught yourself.

So stick around and start to see if you can't agree or relate to some of the information you're going to receive. But more importantly, I want to address your homework before we start getting into the gritty, deep stuff. For instance, I want you to start watching people around you.

Observation is the birth of understanding and without a true sense of observance or a keen eye for noticing the little things, you're not going to pick up on some of these traits. When someone is talking to you, you're going to need to start watching them. Notice how they're standing, note the posture, have you looked at their eyes, what about the overall harmony of their face, and what are they doing with their hands? All of these things need to be running through your mind to really catch what is being conveyed to you. But not just watching their body, note the tones they're using, and the words that they're selecting. These are all going to tell you what sort of body language comes with certain attitudes and emotions. It all ties together and it is all relevant when it comes to understanding body language. So start opening your eyes and let's have a look at what they're trying to say to you.

Are you ready?

Weapons of Mass Induction

Though Sherlock Holmes often touts his use of deductive reasoning, it is actually the opposite that we're going to focus on with you, because right now, you're a student. For those of you that do not know, inductive reasoning starts with observations that slowly build a pattern that you will then form into a hypothesis until it is proven right or wrong. If you're right, then you have a theory.

For example, Kayla touches her hair a lot when she talks to Hot Mike, but not when she's talking to anyone else. So, every time I see Kayla talking to Hot Mike and she's touching her hair, that might be a cue that she likes Hot Mike. So, until I'm proven wrong, I'm certain that I have a theory that when a woman likes a man, she'll touch her hair unconsciously.

Viola, you have just jumped from observation to theory until proven wrong. Of course, when you're Sherlock Holmes level, you'll be using the art of deductive reasoning which starts at a theory and then tested with a hypothesis and observations until you have a conclusion. I think it's time for another example to prove this one to you.

Click Here To Read The Rest of

Body Language 101

What A Person's Body Language Is Really Telling You... And How You Can Use It To Your Advantage

P.S. You'll find many more books like this and others under my name Michele Gilbert.

Don't miss them... here is a short list.

Wicca: The Ultimate Beginners Guide For Witches and Warlocks: Learn Wicca Magic

The Introvert's Advantage: The Introverts Guide To Succeeding In An Extrovert World

Stop Playing Mind Games: How To Free Yourself Of Controlling And Manipulating Relationships

Instant Charisma: A Quick And Easy Guide To Talk, Impress, And Make Anyone Like You

Chakras: Understanding The 7 Main Chakras For Beginners: The Ultimate Guide To Chakra Mindfulness, Balance and Healing

Practicing Mindfulness: Living in the moment through Meditation: Everyday Habits and Rituals to help you achieve inner peace

Adrenal Fatigue: What Is Adrenal Fatigue Syndrome And How To Reset Your Diet And Your Life

Sleep Tight: Overcome Insomnia and Sleep Disorders for a better more restful sleep!

Stop Back Pain Now!: Back Pain Remedies and Treatments so you can live a pain free life!

The Arthritis Pain Cure: How to find Arthritis Pain Relief and live a happy pain free life!

The Headache Pain Cure: How to find Headache Pain Relief and live a happy Pain Free Life!

Stop Panic Attacks and Anxiety Disorders without Drugs Now!: Overcome Panic, Stress and Anxiety and live a happy pain free life!

The Breakup Recovery Guide: Advice for Surviving Heartbreak, Letting Go and Thriving in an exciting new life!

The Friendship Guide to Finding Friends Forever: How to Find, Make and Keep Quality Friendships After your Breakup

How To Stop Being Jealous And Insecure: Overcome Insecurity And Relationship Jealousy

Psychic Development: Your Guide To Unlocking Your Psychic Abilities

So I Am Dating A Psychopath: Now What?

The Mind Of A Sociopath: Your Guide to Understanding The Anti-Social Personality Disorder of Sociopaths

About Michele

Michele Gilbert was born and raised in Brooklyn, New York. Drawn to literature and writing at a young age, she enrolled at Brooklyn College and majored in English. After graduation Michele did not begin writing immediately, instead she embarked on a career in the finance industry and spent the next thirty years on Wall Street.

Serendipity struck when she least expected it. After ending a long-term relationship, Michele found herself lost and unsure what the future held. She began to read books on grief and loss, looking for answers. Those led her to delve deeper into the Law of Attraction and its power. What resulted was remarkable. Not only had she begun to heal, she had also rekindled her former love of writing and discovered her life's purpose.

The years have taken her through many twists and turns, but she learned valuable lessons along the way. Today she publishes books-mostly self-help and metaphysical in nature-and feels compelled to share her knowledge with those facing similar experiences. Her greatest hope is to inspire others and show them ways to overcome adversity and gracefully accept life's inevitable low points.

Going forward, she plans to incorporate more teachings of self-help, finance and meditation. Regular meditation is very beneficial to her progress as she forges a new life. Morning rituals and positive incantations are other practices Michele embraces; they are very restorative in daily life.

As an avid hiker, Michele and fellow club members often hike the picturesque Jersey Pine Barrens. She is a history buff, voracious reader, baseball fanatic and a foodie. She also proudly supports Trout Unlimited-a national non-profit organization dedicated to conserving, protecting and restoring North America's Coldwater fisheries and their watersheds.

Michele currently resides forty minutes from Atlantic City and the Jersey Shore. She makes her home with a Blue Russian rescue cat named Jersey, though she isn't exactly sure who rescued who.

Michele really enjoys publishing books that can make a difference in people's lives. If you have any suggestions or would like to have a specific topic covered in a future book, please send an email to michelegilbertbooks@gmail.com and we will get back to you.

Thanks for reading!